I0203368

the nature
of mountains

poems by
john

Kvasir Books

Kvasir Books

Kvasir, in Norse mythology, a poet and the wisest of all men. Kvasir was born of the saliva of two rival groups of gods, the Aesir and the Vanir, when they performed the ancient peace ritual of spitting into a common vessel. He wandered around teaching and instructing, never failing to give the right answer to a question. Two dwarfs, Fjalar and Galar, who were weary of academics and learning, killed Kvasir and distilled his blood in Odhrǫrir, the magic caldron. When mixed with honey by the giant Suttung, his blood formed mead that gave wisdom and poetic inspiration to those who drank it. —Norse mythology, Encyclopædia Britannica

All photos by the author and photoshopped by the author.

copyright © 2017 John Peterson

ISBN: 978-0-9981469-2-8

All rights reserved. No part of this book may be used or reproduced in any manner whatsoever without written permission, except in the case of quotes for personal use and brief quotations embedded in critical articles or reviews.

Kvasir Books
an imprint of Poetic Matrix Press
www.poeticmatrix.com

the nature
of mountains

acknowledgments

storm in may and *mud slide on glacier point* appeared in Poetic Matrix periodic letter.

for all blue canyons, toward sleep and *break apart* first appeared in the Julian News.

i look up, young girl, aurora y alexandria, mt. laguna, our dark season, and *together* appeared in *Two Races One Face Two Faces One Race* with Thomas Gayton.

how far back and *double doors* were written during a month long retreat at Dorland Mountain Arts Colony, Temecula, CA in 1995.

early morning walk, half dome and full moon, for ansel adams, and *uzumite—grizzly bear* were presented at the Yosemite Centennial Celebration Concert in The Great Lounge of the Ahwahnee Hotel September 2, 1990, sponsored by the National Park Service.

Thanks to James Downs for his friendship and editorial help. And of course thanks to Laurene, Devon and Kiirsti for their inspiration.

contents

dedication

poetry is a forsaking of power
for beauty, truth and love

the ocean above
the fire below
and all of earth's
creatures live
in between

swaying and moving
with all her forces
above and within

laurene

the nature
of mountains

leaving

wilderness in the city

the place where possum and skunk walk
where hawk circles and cries out

where winter clouds overcome
the reputation of beach and sun

a small spread of blue
the slightest touch of a breeze

everything else asphalt and steel
rough side of buildings and planted trees

nothing made before the first necklace
of fertile beads chipped from black rock

and flung out at the wild creature that
would join the wild creature within

making a looping circle   recognition of cycles
the goddess without voice
here before all this asphalt and steel

basho's pond

today in the late afternoon
with the sun giving off white rays
and a curious wind blowing

i sit and refocus my perceptions

eyes removed from buildings
and hard surfaces   ears release
cars and the sound of sirens

brain releases city and they all
with a sideways look pick up
the wild flute and guitar tabla harp
and tamboura and join the mind and
heart in the seeking of wild

a strange and peculiar waiting
hearing

basho's pond

on the edge of

listening

there

there

in the date palm

yellow sunlight swaying
circular
motion

wind and

                              sound and

             mind

                                     given back

instantaneous

        where wild danced out

                      at me

chollas lake

there is a treeline at chollas lake
the upper most canopy the dominate melodic line

long slender leaves   dark green
with black at their base

a smell in the nose of curried leaves
tree trunk with large patches of bark peeling

the grey source a softness that holds the trunk
to ground dissolution into the water's melodic line

mud hens at the edge of the lake

blue feathers green leaves in the air of eucalyptus
exacting ripples in mud light soil scattered with leaves
blown brown and lacy soil laced with rocks of uniform size

blue edge of water   never repeated melodic line

young girl on a pink bike rides on the rocks
and says hi!

young slender eucalyptus electrified body

towards sleep

approaching sleep not yet deep
animals enter deer and coyote
possum and coon raven and jay

they cross the line that ineffable place
that is protected without our
knowing why

and all through the night out there
not in the dream these creatures
cavort and play wrestling
in the leaves and running wildly
across the porch at my feet

tadpoles

—for devon

last night the pond was the size of a small hat
ten or fifteen of you holding on enough water
only to cover your back and keep the sun off

foot print of coon and coyote dog and deer
and small bird circling down from reed covered
bank across cracked mud and soggy bottom

you squirm hoping against time and biology that
legs will sprout in time a race against summer sun
large and small creatures an eternity of narrow chances

one of you moves from runny mud back legs
near strong enough unsure that this is the time
but choices going fast as noonday

feeble hop out of dwindling mud toward
parched landscape that may offer escape
from the certainty of diminished water

you will make it if time and biology
cross precisely

break apart

i feel like i'm slowly losing that crack
in my chest the one where sweet wind blows

if i stay long enough hawk or raven will come
first just circling then maybe there in the tree

if i can break apart and crumble like stone
gone to seed i'll feel those wildly beating wings

fly through

leaves

leaves in planes light in front
flat like windows dark behind

tunnel-like
and in the distance

movement from a spirit that tangles
the leaves

one time

she told me one time that the most
profound thing is to talk to trees

i remember sitting beneath that
great blue oak playing my clay flute   I've
never played in five octaves

dimension

in mountains

lost in mountains
       extracted from books

i'll meet you on the trail
hidden by the bracken fern
and we shall breath

"a"

there is a clear "a" through the colter pine
middle "e" through black oak leaves
a whole where birds fly

the color of night
through the hairs on my arms
and on your lips

and only in these can i find the sound i seek

tao

all i hear is a high whine
zummmm
from the wings of a ruby red throat
and lime dripped body
of hummingbird
feeding

to movement

reach your hand into still air
and pull it
dig your fingers into damp ground
and bring it with you
spread your arms across the ridge
and make it rolling
place your hands at the oak tree's root
and raise it with you
send your chi upon the grass
and feel it bending
give your red eye to the hawk's wing
and learn its calling
make your heart the same with the land
and you'll be green

feather

two times at my feet
the feather of raven and
two in the coulter pine this morning

calling the universe inside

for all blue canyons*

"Many Marchers said they had awoken
from consciousness to find butterflies
fluttering about their lips.
Some even believed they had been dead
drowned, and that the butterflies had
brought them back to life."
—— from Satanic Verses by Salmon Rushdie

Yes, this is a fine place.

The D-13 caterpillar blade howls into the deerbrush
    bursting it from the ground like a boil exploding
    the blue atmosphere stained with diesel smoke
    a dark acrid haze.

Nothing here no great Black Oak   Bull Pine,
    no fresh mountain water
    diving into granite pools.

400 ten wheelers roll on the head of coyote
    its continuous yelping causing eardrums
    to vibrate like a child screaming.

Canyon slopes are ripped open sending dust clouds
    over the eyes of astronomers and tourists
    until we can't see trash disappear
    into metaphorical land fills.

Neighbors given a free pass to watch 3 million
    tons of garbage heap up; old bicycles, vases broken,
    frayed chairs, rotting food, plastic containers,
    bottle upon bottle, Campbell soup cans line the canyon
    walls in place of buckbrush, bottlebrush and sage.

Ansel Adams' eyes open, John Muir comes awake.

3 Million people line the canyon slopes with dust
   covered eyes, ears vibrating to the diesel motor,
   blood satiated with acrid smoke, throwing
   arms and legs into Caterpillar graves.

Near the roadside a single orange monarch butterfly
   moves across the canyon, her wings at first tiny
   as they beat in the blue air, then become huge
   as they envelope the whole canyon.

*Blue Canyon in San Diego County proposed as
   a trash dump site defeated by local protest.

how far back

how far back must i go
to find the pattern in the falling
rain on ellen's cabin

to some primordial rhythm man
putting down a beat
to which i hear only one
infinitesimally small part

dropping down on the shingled roof
of ellen's cabin
in the evening light rain
on dorland mountain

double doors

outside the double doors
tangled vine draped from the roof
to the oak trunk
on elegant waves of woody stem
barren and the leaves reach out

you made a large intricate web
two feet across strands and slopes
long stringers attached to the eves
and the woody vine

you furry orange shape waiting
in the center of your work as the
rain and cold work on the surroundings

i wait looking occasionally to see you
live your world but it seemed in suspension
waiting for the cold to recede the rain to cease
and the sun to bring you some morsel

but it nevere came you never moved
finally caught left silent in your own web
twisted and cold

left in the ignominious fate of the design
of your own world but left either trapped
in your design or finally the inevitable comes
and you rest in your handiwork

wrapped in the strange working of your love

not here and here

still and not still
silent and not silent

buddha says nirvana is not here and here

listen and the ear travels across the meadow
high up into the pine and deep
below the oak

silence spreads like fingers on skin
coyote jogs onto the meadow
a doe and two faun stand with us
eye to eye and then leap up hill

ground squirrel and grey squirrel
scouting seeds on the forest floor
a store for them a worker for the oak
doing and not doing

raccoon leaves the circle of light
oily movement perfect and not perfect

the night a great yin absorbing the world
long and deep without definition
until raccoon brings oily movement

owl a hole in the mind
and fifteen coyotes the calling
of a primal people
inside coyote god

your feathers long and golden
sitting in the top branches of the grey snag
three days six fool wings with the note
of the flute through the black oak leaves

bird people allow the orange wing
give away

not here and here
not here and here

mixed up

we are all mixed up
us and you
how do we know where
the boundaries are
the wind through the hairs
on my arm

we are here

we are here through
all the changes
we leave our signs for
any who care to see
but we do not leave them
to be seen

your mountain

i look up

i look up and the vulture
passes overhead

i am quickly connected to
the hills of my home
and to you

my first impulse was to
say to you "look the vulture
flies with us"

but you are in san diego
and i am here in managua

young girl

here the young girl   hand on hip
legs askew
eyes like coffee trees on la montaña

i kiss your lips and su madre
rolls over and warms the stones
in place shifts the dark wing
that i sleep wrapped in

your dark eyes and su madre
call in la montaña of my
sleep in the afternoon
and the low sun

aurora y alexandria

before i leave nicaragua
i want to draw
a line between the full open
smile you gave me when we
first met

and the heart filled with sadness
when i left

i leave you stay but i have
seen our heart broken together
and i want you to
be happy again   full of
hope and a future you
can trust

not the war not the boy
in the volcanic mountains with
the gun

i won't forget and i'll
stay with you 'til the time
when alexandria can smile
all the time like the smile
on the face of my little boy

mt. laguna

almost autumn on the slopes of mt. laguna
burnt rancheria pinyon loop cosmic eye bright
as the night fire makes the ring as two
we stand grounded in sky

below across the road forming mexican singer
around the fire that makes the ring
five or six tents take up the camping site
children yell out playing and running all
manner of games they rise out of the dark
light by lanterns on poles and ropes between trees

grown ones at tables in groups cooking
carne asada and cervesa is served conversation
muted the music reaches the first star on
plumes of plum smoke

to the far right around the fire that makes
the ring around the stone she stands framed
by his eyes she stands for his hands as he
splits the oak log with a long handled ax

further below boisterous as beer cans are
tossed in a heap horse high laughter leaps
the air off its drifting course
three men who would be friends to the fire
that makes the ring talk until the hour
when satellites and comets strain for
the eye of magic here in the early
beginnings of cities set amongst jeffrey pine
and coulter black oak and white fir

choosing we have come choosing we will travel
ten thousand years to our homes tomorrow set
in the city that is in canyons set in the city
that is set in hills and in river beds set in the
space between tall trees and loud voices

and is only below the sun and is only within
the wind that comes through ocean or desert and
is only made wet and cold by great clouds
that stretch the length of mexico and only sits upon
these billion tons of rock traveling through space
and would take years to reach the first star on
plumes of plum smoke

and around the fire that makes the ring we sit
grounded in sky and our love rises on
plumes of plum smoke to reach the first star
and returns on the wings of a feathered serpent

dark season

we keep finding small places that let the
smell of herbs come through

rosemary before its put in the black skillet
with potatoes onions and black pepper

basil oregano and cilantro growing on the roof
top deck where the sound of pigeons and sunsets
fill the sky and early morning bells
from the methodist steeple
stand out against the snow covered peaks
of the cuyamacas

the source of rain in the spider plant
the deep smell of burning oak
eucalyptus both wet and shining and played out in smoke

this is the season the bear sleeps where you and i
slowly give in and lay front to back like spoons in
a velvet embrace

our meeting

long ribbons of soil urns of lust
solemn and dusty rain without ending

mountain tops in the gold mouth of dusk
our love a memory of secret drumming

i wake some mornings forgetful
having not met you in our lovers dream

going about my day with the dream not forged
not taken into this world that is so hard on dreams

our meeting was in a dream long
before i held you in my arms the first time

i look for you when i lay on our futon
touch your body ask to meet you in the time of dreams

to renew our love and let that love flow
from our bed into the foolish world be must inhabit

until our power is great enough to make a change
so that our dream and the world are the same

prayer beads

we touch a sweet wind that blows
when a holding like a sigh is released

satin straining against your breast
eating the space around you

felt hammer vibration in the morning air
circling you like bees in the garden

water from your eyes strung
a sacred string of prayer beads

waiting

window open   salt
up the hill

wet in my face
deep in
cold only for a moment

all night

morning first light
comes then you

on me and what is
full around me gets
fuller still

i make a gesture
and wait for a response
from the 4th world
and remain

wrestling love

flirting in the darkened light
i watch the gleam mischievous and sensual
stray from your glance

my aloofness holds for awhile
but we are brought closer
by the deep red burn on your breast

reaching back wrestling love
desire settling on us drowning us
holding our separate lives together

bound in a continuous unfolding pattern
where the charge of love holds us
and all things together

yosemite journal

uzumite—grizzly bear

compress the genesis
of yosemite
into a few precious seconds
a bone chilling
glacial movement
the insides of which covers
the earth around
and then
streams out
a song in the shroud
ecstatic
hiss

vernal falls in autumn

it's the
wall
that catches me
many faces
cuts and turns

the ledges that take the long
fists
of water coming over the top and
get smoothed and polished and
then accept the sunlight and
give the deep
glossy
surface a
burnt red and
black granite
patina

john muir describes the long fists of water
dropping off of yosemite falls and then
either breaking up into long streamers
that turn into a fine exacting mist or   making
the complete fall   give off a sonorous clap
when they hit shaped surfaces below   with
his eyes and description i see the same
here   as the fists form about one third

down
and create long streaming
tails
on their way

at two thirds down
many come apart
disintegrating
into so many particles of
mist
swirling
back and upward

as they catch sunlight and
give off the cool image of
celestial
wings hovering about the
waterscape

the remaining
fists
gather
velocity and
head for three curving ledges below

the first ledge starts
far up the south
side   and in a
long   easy   curve
stops on the lower north edge

the fists
that catch this ledge
slap
with a high   quick sound
the water running quickly to
a shelf and into the pool
below
fast   high   and
dancing sounds

the second ledge
starts out lower then the first
and runs across the
face
in an
easy   melodic   line

the fists
that are caught here splat
loudly and echo against the back wall

sending spray out a dozen
channels to the lower red
rock and the wide
pool

the third ledge
is low and long
and runs gradually from
side to side a thick
protruding lip
it meets the fists
that leap far out and if they land at
the central point
a wide curved dish
the sound is a deep
thrump

that sets vibration
into rock
the water jumps out over the side and
in switching sequence hollowed out
surface impression sheets down the rock
wall with a vision of hand held hips and
the high facade of the pipes

all this from broken
fragment
water that comes over the top
and then starts a
journey transformed
through granite light and a long fall
into something that clears the mind
and opens the eye to see

waterline

i stop and look up to a view
of a cloud line high up on yosemite's
granite cliffs

it was startling
like looking up at the surface of a lake
like water had been magically held back

it was all very simple and peaceful
and easy somehow

early morning walk
—laurene

you and i go for an early morning walk
night silence still in the tree tops
a crust of ice holding the edge of
water
below yosemite falls
our limbs waking like the douglas fir

granite rocks in yosemite creek
giving off mid-night dark
chill   our ears and cheeks with a
sweet morning sting

we walk and breathe in quiet cadence
and meet the
valley morning

rounding a soft pad of earth
that leads to a small secluded meadow
still hidden by tall conifer
from morning sun
we catch each others eyes to signal
silence

without movement
we see
two dark figures head and antlers
down
into
the tall grass

we move quietly
to a system of granite boulders
and sit

one figure larger darker and older
raises his head
and shows a rack with eight points
his body muscled and agile

he moves
 in a precise gait
alive
through grass
and the lightening shadows

the other figure   smaller lighter with a rack
of four points   left his gaze on the old one
a moment too long
entered the other's space
a breath too close

and was jumped back
by a sharp swing of
eight points
and a smooth gaze

i play
sounds
on my clay flute

both figures look up   adjust brown
and black lined ears to locate
rivulet of notes

bring their eyes to our spot
hold for a moment   and then return to the
tall grass

soon the older one moves
  in a precise gait
to the end of the meadow
where the sun is touching
the young one
moves along at a distance

their
gaze the
whole meadow

their breath
a flooding of light
scent of creatures
rocks and trees

for ansel adams
—the photograph of siesta lake

we find it
30 years later
the trunk of the grey snag leaned over
but unmistakable
the rocks
that make the same stone steps
and the fir trunk in the right
corner

all week stepping inside the various
scenes
most seen on post cards
and a million home videos
slides and prints
vistas that stretch out and become
almost impossible to take in
our imagination
there where he stood trampled
by so many

but here we find
the stone where he set his
tripod
we search the lake
and surrounding mountain for the
right spot

what should frame the left side
how high up the treeline

should the fir be
in the frame or out

what makes the view
work   how much water in
the foreground

our hair raises and a
smiles rides in our belly

we move to the spot
focused in our eye and
camera

check the ground the
granite stones and green
grass stepped on

looking up we rise
inside him and see
out
as he sees

yosemite valley

coyote coyote
large circle
eye to eye
using paved trail through

the meadow you pause
tail high nose toward the
ground right paw up

poised waiting short quick
leap a moment to kill
a moment to swallow

noonday passes

the merced

all day i walk while the river beats its rhythm
in the other direction   surely toward its own kind

i struggle to let my mind free of preoccupation
now and then we all sprang out
a rock that had wings   a tree that regurgitated water all
around   a great
piece of granite that blew off yesterday
the crowed feet of deer   red clouds breathing
out of el capitan   tissack* and her dog
flat sheets of ice that were held up

scandinavian grandfather who
walked with me

i'll dream tonight and if i'm lucky   for a time
the ways of men and women will be gone

*ahwahneechee princess whose dog and tear stained face
 are etched on half dome

yosemite again

in yosemite again   this time in early spring
bridalvail like a young bride white train
blowing across polished black granite

the quiet of the valley set inside
the constant roar of flowing water

remnants of late winter white snow
breaks up the new greenness of the valley floor
the merced flows at my feet   spreads

through the soles of my shoes and up my legs

i listen and the white sound of the river
carries sounds i have heard in many places

my twin boys born in a water storm
my son's birth from water into music
my daughter's first sound out of water

the sound of water drawn up to the sky   gathered
in storms and given as rain to the high country

water rushing together into quiet places
or the rapids of lives   making all these sounds

dogwood summer

outside my double doors
a family of dogwood
stands in the coming fall season

inside and outside the air is the same
still in the afternoon
with the sun gone behind glacier point

dogwood family begins
the first stage of change toward winter
a few leaves barely curling brown

pulling ever so slowly
from the outward expanse of summer
to a deep place in the interior of their world

storm in may

may storm
raced through uzumite all night
the merced flowed over banks returning valley floor
to its original flood plane

at dawn the results were apparent
on the faces of campers and residents

secrets everywhere
between wake and sleep
humans and the wild at an edge

all day we watch and wait as water
rises or recedes

in late afternoon the road is opened   the human tribe
assembles to go to their homes with stories of the
great mother's sudden show of beauty

i bike to the base of lower yosemite falls
and start up the path

ground shudders
yosemite creek's banks pushed high
debris scattered over grey polished boulders

belly tightens
brownish water more than i have seen
falls hard

walking over the bridge   spray beats at my face
blowing out as always but further
reverberating rock bends my knees
edges of all kinds are lost
recrossing i turn my back to the torrent

that crumbles granite walls

rush of water breaking down stream
hammers my back
point of sky at granite line across the valley

half moon of blue like an invitation
stays open for a moment
then falling water stinging points of iron spray
mouth open icy pins at my throat

sound rumbling earthly glory
roaring wild steel slick granite skin of surrounding
wet wall surface infused in morning light

mauling water boulder pools in raging
red flush sculpted piece of broken rock and wood

whole trees smashed kindling golden white splinters
against newly broken granite surface
laughing belly merging lost in water

falling white screaming high pitched boiling love
of the cold dark hollow of our voices in concert

mouth open reverent rolling sexual wonder
legs tremble sway and stumble
face stung cold and bitten

back turned to hardened water hidden in mid-morning

my tribe waiting to exit this wildness that has us
whether we wish it or not

waiting for warm summer days where we can walk
safe in our human fragileness

blooming dogwood white flower petal tells us this storm
is at the cusp of winter's final going

and the glowing days that are ahead

mud slide on glacier point

our movement stops
we travel across soaked
forest floor up vertical granite
3000 feet dancing on

contemplation point

roaring long tunnel of water
turned loose in a rage
of emotionless fury beyond
our ordinary sound and
hearing in the storm
that has left us stranded

looking up stair step falls
clear icy water now a dark
peculiar mass of rock and
mud slewing into our midst

watching in wonder
and apprehension we spread
out across nerve and muscle
viscera and instinct old
as white granite
falling in front of us

two days later
the glory has changed
to sunlight on new snow
we walk softly
with cautious intent
looking and listening

sisters and brothers
—kiirsti

twisting sturdy in winter
covers the white faced buddha

water finding low places
between grass and sky

i yell join wind brothers
between straight trunks

moving along swift green
treeline to treeline

dodging boulders in and out
looking ready

the ground opens up   out jumps
a small man in stripped coat

quickly quickly turn you head
red tail filters yellow particles

drops message into your dreaming
place   did you get it

your whole life now moves closer
to foot high sisters with yellow droopy

tops set up in the meadow
by the hundreds

no change—uzumite

in the changing direction
this spire stands out

the sun in a new place
and there are gothic elements

i blink many times and shadows
sheer off high mountains

i whirl on the path
and arms reach up from high granite walls

i standing still
the ground rotates and black is bold

i turning unsteady
and coyote leaps out

i make a bed of pine needles
and the slope drops off one thousand feet

i wake from dreaming
and quickly light is in place

i go from my place to the other
and all the deer are thankful

i become the center
and everything is food for grey squirrel

i think about home
and valley walls become partial

i cease to think
and the dawn starts out

i cease to see
and bears bed down or arise

adventures in weather

Tuolumne Meadows

A few years ago our family spent a month camping in Tuolumne Meadows, 9000 feet high in the Sierra Nevada Mountains, the emerald jewel of Yosemite National Park. Camping in the months of June/July at such an elevation is always a challenge, but the locals said this year was particularly rough. The weather didn't even turn to spring until after the 4th of July. Tent camping in such conditions with a one year old and a three year old becomes a particular adventure.

After driving all day from Palomar Mountain in San Diego County we arrived in Fresno at 5:00 in the evening to pick up the friends who were to accompany us. On impulse we decided to make the four hour drive to the high country that night rather than wait until morning.

We pulled into the Tuolumne Meadows Campground around 10:00. The air was cold, the ground wet and snow covered, and here, after the long drive with young children, the bottom dropped out. This was the wrong place for a family right now. The thought of putting up a tent was the wrong thought. We stopped, took a deep breath to collect ourselves and bring our thoughts to a more reasonable plan. A tent cabin at Tuolumne Lodge—with a fire —was the right plan, and so we settled in for the night. It turned out we settled in for a few days, cozy and warm, eating meals at the Lodge Dining Room and the Lembert Dome picnic area. It rained and remained seriously cold all week.

We might as well have called this "adventures in weather." In fact at one point we did; this was not a vacation but an adventure and so we operated accordingly, deciding each day if we should continue our stay. Remaining both flexible in our itinerary, as we could not be sure from day to day what we could do, and developing a keenness for the new and unexpected that adventures always bring, we began to settle down. The weather came, all of it; thunderstorms, rain, hail, snow, and cold—serious cold — yes, and a day or two of sun now and then, to which we were thankful.

After our friends left we moved from the Lodge to a large 6-person tent, tried to say warm and dry with young kids, and deal with the varieties of weather. Clear in the morning, cloudy in the afternoon, rain, clear nights, or some variation, was the mark of each day.

One afternoon, the storm became serious; huge thunderheads, lightening strikes all over the high country, hail in large quantities, and snow—enough so that the Rangers closed the road on either end of the Meadow. The temperature dropped and we hightailed it for the Lodge for the night. Weather, weather!

Was there anything besides weather? Yes, Devon fell into Tenya Lake, clothes and all; Kiirsti fell off —or into—Lembert dome, skinning her nose; and Laurene was a trooper. We also had some nice hikes in the Meadow and evenings around the camp fire under the cold clarity of stars.

While talking with Laurene about our eating habits at such a high, cold elevation, it became clear that places, conditions, and activities have a distinct bearing on the kind of consciousness one cultivates. "State specific consciousness" was the term I used several years ago to designate the kind of awareness that revolves around specific circumstances.

Here we eat more, drink hot herbal teas, coffee and Kahlua to warm the interior, and generally bulk up to deal with the rather harsh conditions. Our consciousness extends inward and outward in particular ways. We do focus more on what we call survival or conservation issues, but this is too simplistic. Along with this comes heart concerns for the others in the group, their well-being, comfort, outlook, etc., plus the close camaraderie that occurs when dealing with difficult external conditions. The attention to the surroundings, first dealing with weather and the possibility of rain, cold, snow, etc. turns to a greater appreciation for the beautiful play of wind, clouds, sun, and storms on Mt. Lyell and the surrounding granite peaks.

A cold wind on the face, the power of Lodgepole Pine, Red Fir, Marmot, Sierra Chickaree and the other beings here who deal with these elements year after year, gives us a more pronounced respect for the ability of all of us to adapt, survive, and find the extraordinary no matter where we are. The consciousness out there takes in all of this and more.

During breaks in the rain and snow, and with the proper layered clothing, we find time to enjoy the vigorous wonder of the place. With Devon and Kiirsti tucked in the bike trailer we ride through the Meadow singing our song, "Oh we're riding along, on Tuolumne Road, everywhere that we go(ad) there's another pot ho(ad)." Our rhymes are forced but the exhilaration comes easily.

The consciousness that turns inside deals also with issues of well-being, but again this passes as we adapt behavior to the conditions, secure the interior spaces and insure that all will be well. Finally, the interior consciousness curves into old sources, deep historical and primordial places of remembrance; how it was, what the ancestral conditions were.

We reflect on the native people who made this their summer home; who trekked the trails from Mono Lake to the Valley floor, bundled up against the changing conditions.

Sitting with our hot coffee and Kahlua around the fire after the children are finally wrapped in sleeping bags, we also recall our ancestors, bundled as they were against the harshness of the Scandinavian weather, an ancient fire warming their front, the dark cold night at their back. Their stories are coded still in tissues, cells, memories, and associations. A calmness comes from knowing that we, all of us, have shared these times, human to human over millennia.

Finally the connection, at a core level, of our shared place with the beings of the natural world, Lodgepole, Marmot, Golden Eagle, Junco learning from the inside of their ways, recognizing how closely our lives and theirs are intertwined.

Our respect for the wild world grew in these weeks as did our personal humility. We gained a different sense of what life in the city means. Dealing with small children in such harsh conditions as these is taxing beyond what is comfortable. We'll enjoy the comforts of our home upon our return to the city. Hopefully our critique of the city, and the rise of industrial and technical development, will, in the future, be more pointed and will not lapse into blanket condemnations with some romanticized vision of living in the wild.

The question of how to protect the wild world, and partake in its wisdom remains, as well as how to make the cities more in tune with nature and yet not lose the comforts that cities can bring. We'll come to these questions with more equanimity I think.

We have gained a deeper appreciation for the wildness of the wild and recognize that we must come to it with our strength intact, meeting it with vigor, preparation, and a mature resolve.

Now, no matter what fire we warm ourselves in front of, this adventure, high in the cold light of Tuolumne Meadows, will fill our conscious remembrance. We draw from a submerged, hidden place, set down in this primordial encounter.

hide

hide inside a tree for awhile
a lodgepole would be ok

don't come out 'til the
madness dissolves like

snow on the subalpine
meadow

be sure and ask first

author biography

John is the author of three previous books of poetry including; *News of the Day, dark hills and wild mountains* and *Two Races One Face Two Faces One Race* with Tomás Gayton. He is the publisher and editor of Poetic Matrix Press and Poetic Matrix Press' online Forever Journal and Poets Comment into the World blogs. As the publisher of Poetic Matrix Press, a literary small press, he has published more than 50 books of poetry and prose from writers across the country and around the world. He has read from his poetry, lectured and taught at: the University of California San Diego; California State University San Diego; California State University Fresno; University for Humanistic Studies, Del Mar, CA; The Writing Center in San Diego; Palomar College San Marcos; Merced High School; Yosemite National Park including the Yosemite Centennial Celebration at the Ahwahnee Hotel in 1990; Barnes and Noble in Berkeley; Ina Coolbirth Circle in Orinda; performances include venues in many communities including Managua, Nicaragua.

Information on Poetic Matrix Press can be found at www.poeticmatrix.com.

www.ingramcontent.com/pod-product-compliance
Lightning Source LLC
Chambersburg PA
CBHW022037090426
42741CB00007B/1105